SALLY ODGERS LISA STEWART

# Bushland Lullaby

A Scholastic Press book from Scholastic Australia

In the sunlit gully, green and wide
Where secret nooks are fine to hide
In a soft and grassy snuggly nest
Little *bandicoot* comes to rest.

Snug in the hollow of an old gum tree
When the morning light is blithe to see

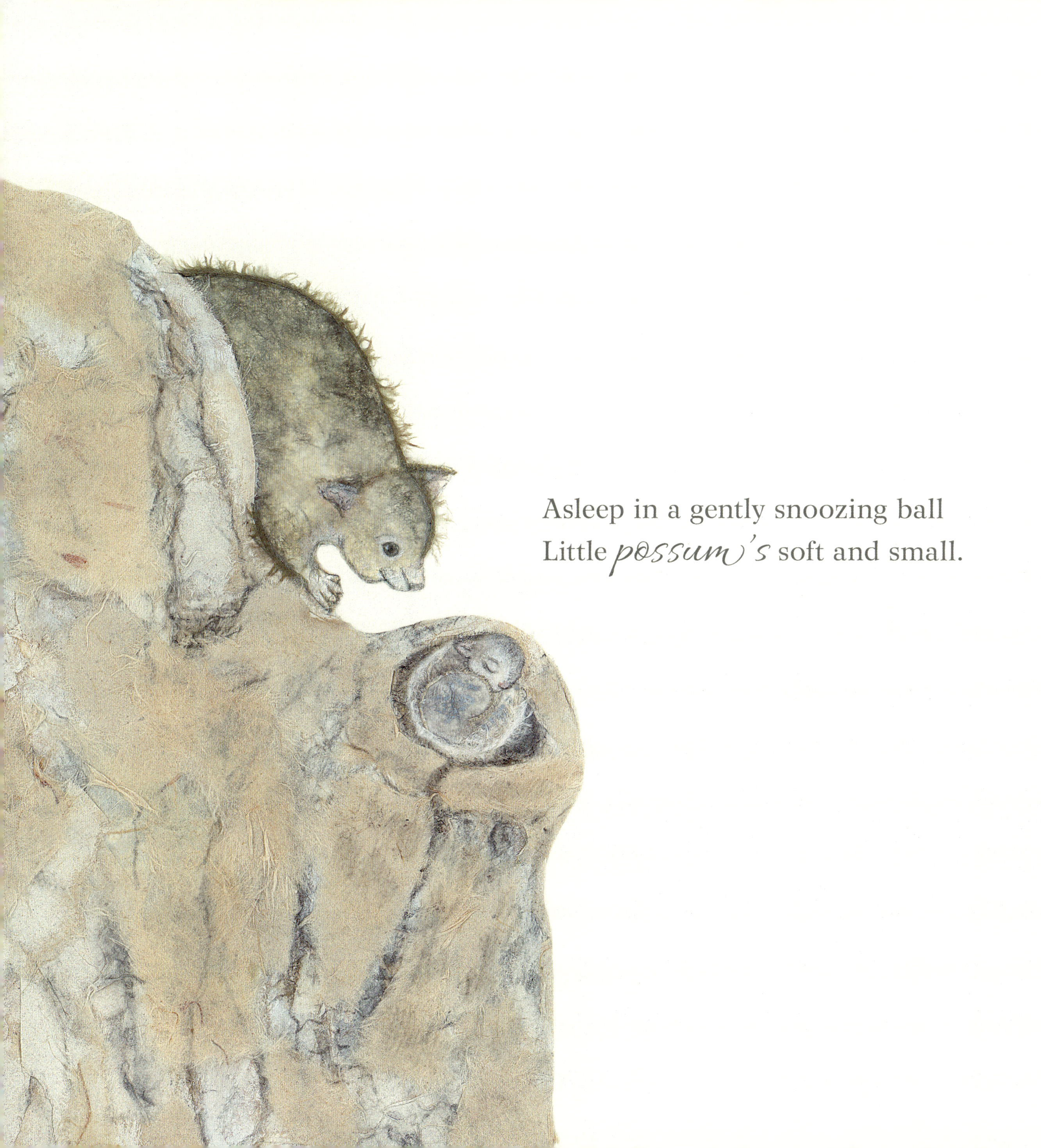

Asleep in a gently snoozing ball
Little *possum*'s soft and small.

In a merry creek where the currents run
Where eddies dance with winking sun
Curled in a burrow so safe and deep
Little *platypus* lies asleep.

There in a tropical mangrove stand
Where salty mud is warm as sand
In hushing waters by the river's smile
Don't wake little *crocodile*.

On the scribbly trunk of a leaning tree
So still, so quiet, he's hard to see

In the place he thinks is bushland's best
Little *goanna* clings to rest.

There's a lonely island in the sea
Where breakers sing when the wind blows free
In a pebbled nest out of water's reach
Little *seagull*'s on the beach.

On a shivering island clad with snow
Where the ocean kisses icy floes
In a stony nest with her mother close
Little *penguin* may safely doze.

In the wattle grove, under dappled skies
When the drifting clouds fly soft and high
Through the afternoon of restful hours
Little *wallaby* comes to drowse.

Down in the bush where the gum trees thrive
Where the lazy breeze brings scents alive
In the lofty fork of an ancient tree
Little *koala* goes to sleep.

Burrowed into an earthy mound
In the summer day when the sun bakes down
In a twisty tunnel and cosy bed
Little *wombat* rests his head.

Hung like fruit in a tropical park
In bundles strangely plump and dark
When the sunset's pink and the cricket zings
Little *fruit bat's* wrapped in wings.

On the windy plain beyond the town
Where grass grows rough and rustling brown
The sun gives way to cool moonbeams
And little *emu's* chasing dreams.

In the wild red desert where the sun's alight
Or the sky flings stars in a winter's night
In the shade of a rock pile's ancient calm
Little *dingo's* safe from harm.

Under sparkling skies, by friendly seas
In your own backyard, by the rivers and trees
Think of this when it's time for *bed* . . .

You're not the only *sleepy head.*

SALLY ODGERS LISA STEWART

# Rainforest Lullaby

A Scholastic Press book from Scholastic Australia

Gleeful laughter rings at dawn
As kookaburra greets the morn
But when the sky with stars is touched
*Kookaburra's* laugh is hushed.

Where misty forest canopies
Shroud the boles of hollow trees
Snuggled safe till the sun slips down
*Ringtail possum's* sleeping sound.

In the drowsing tropic scene
*Tree frog's* clinging green-on-green
Fluttered wings go drifting by
To share their peaceful lullaby.

In their den through noontide heat
With tummies round and twitching feet
The *devil pups* all sweetly sleep
Snuggled in a furry heap.

Cassowary in the dusk
Settles in a nest of brush
Chicks all dressed in feathered stripes
Cuddle with him through the night.

*Water dragon* haunts the creek
Basking on a stone to sleep
Or lounges on a leafy vine
Dreaming of an ancient time.

Of forest nights *Boobook* is king
Coasting silent through the dim
Back to sleepy boughs he comes
To roost when all the hunting's done.

A hollow log is cool and snug
*Echidna's* full of ants and bugs
Dozing through the steamy hours
And heavy swish of tropic showers.

Sugar glider's up all night
Gliding through the soft moonlight
When golden sun replaces moon
*Sugar glider's* resting soon.

In forests old or ever young
The *gentle* airs of life are sung
With creaking boughs
and *rushing rain* . . .

You'll hear the *lullaby* again.

SALLY ODGERS LISA STEWART

# Outback Lullaby

A Scholastic Press book from Scholastic Australia

Outback babies close their *eyes*
To *dream* the outback lullaby.

Scurry, scurry through the night
But *bilby* sleeps when sun is bright.

Hidden in a rocky den
*Spotted quoll's* asleep again.

When cuddled to a mulga tree
*Frilled-neck lizard's* hard to see.

Stripy *emu chicks* may rest.
Dad protects them in the nest.

Into Mother's pouch to snooze
Clambers small red *kangaroo*.

As the sunset spreads its glow
Little *brolga's* dancing slow.

The chatter in the tree sounds sweet
Sleepy *rainbow lorikeet.*

The outback hums with twilight sounds.

*Numbat* dreams of termite mounds.

Beneath a sheltered slab of stone
*Thorny devil's* quite at home.

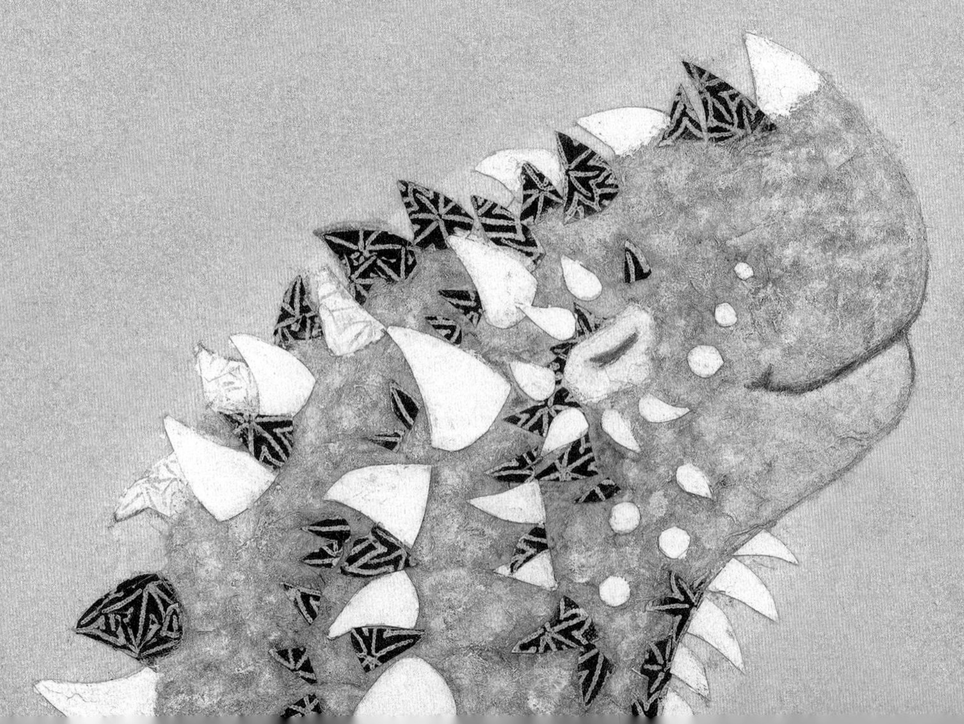

Now my darling, close your eyes
To dream of *outback lullabies*.

SALLY ODGERS LISA STEWART

# Ocean Lullaby

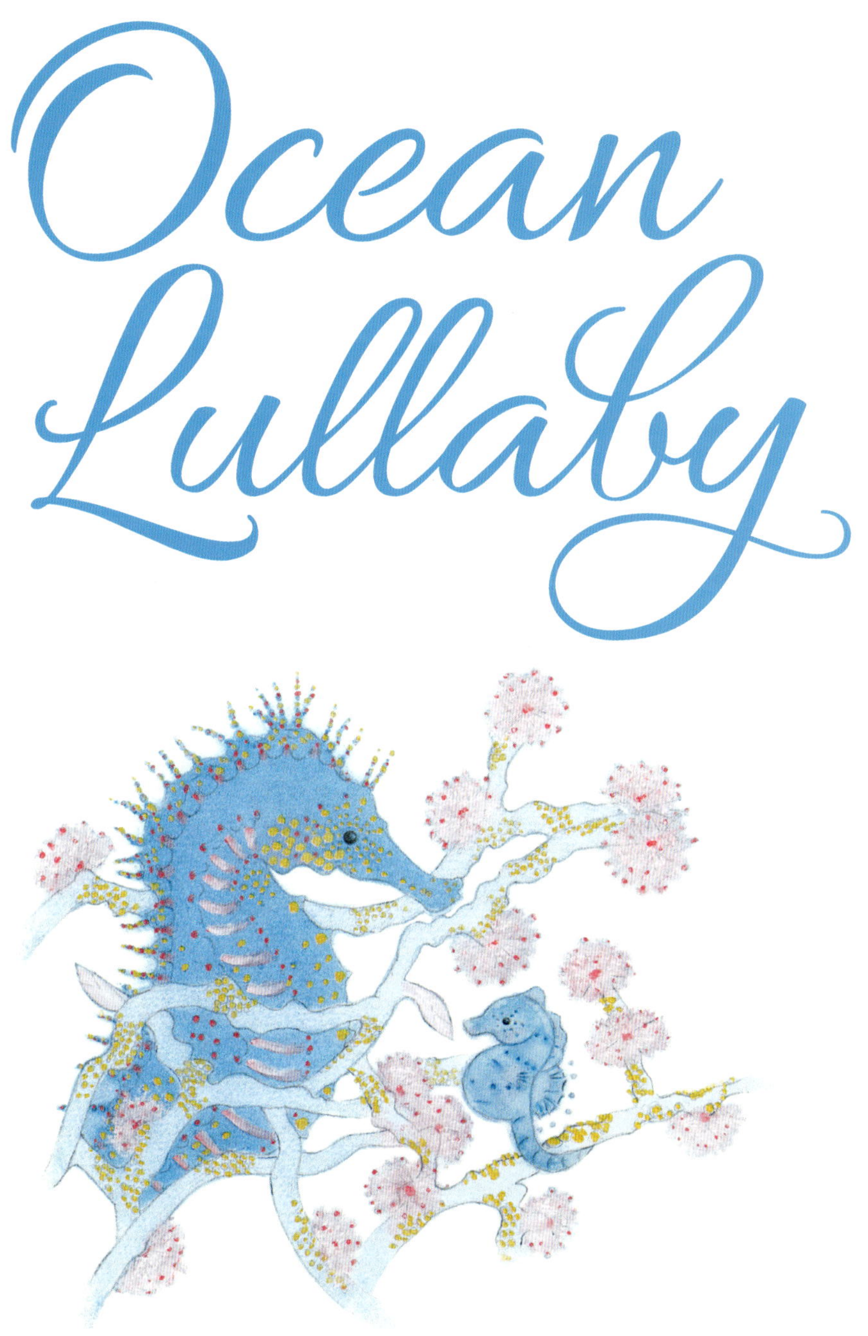

A Scholastic Press book from Scholastic Australia

Ocean babies in the *deep*
Waves are *rocking* them to sleep.

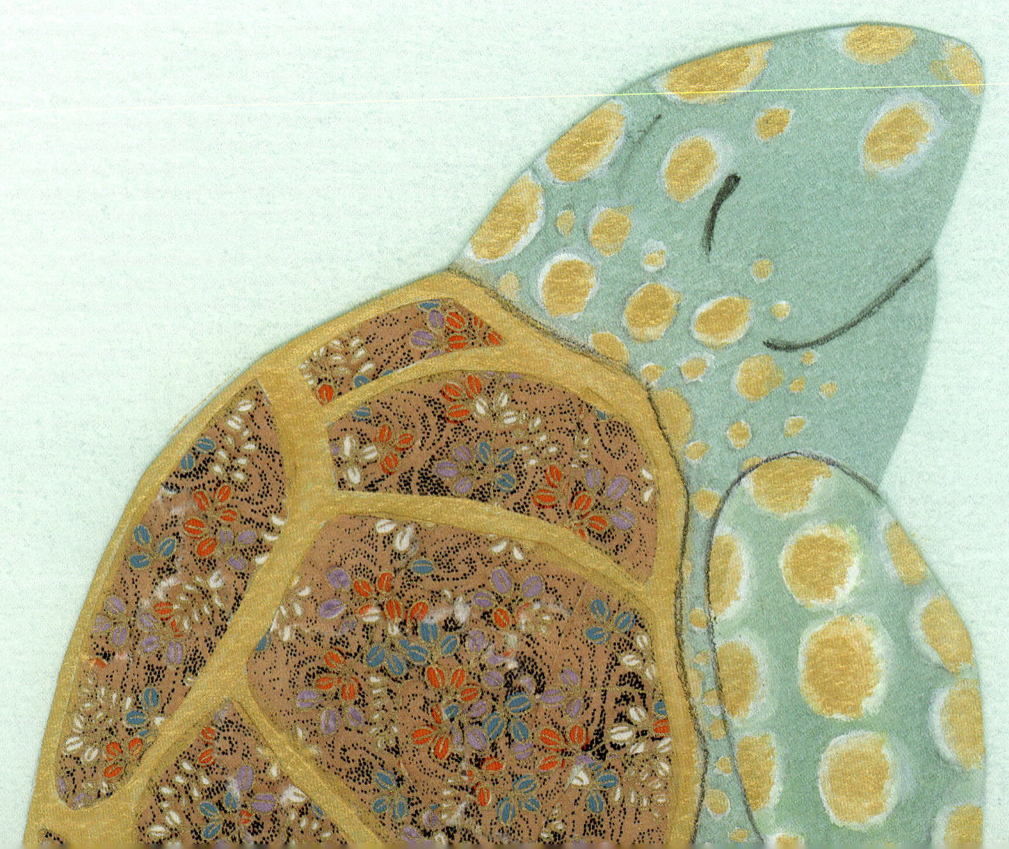

Little *turtle* likes to wedge
In an underwater ledge.

*Cuttlefish*, so silent, shy
In the shallows drifting by.

Baby *seahorse* in the tide
Finds a quiet place to hide.

Drowsy *whale* calf seems to smile
Swimming by his mother's side.

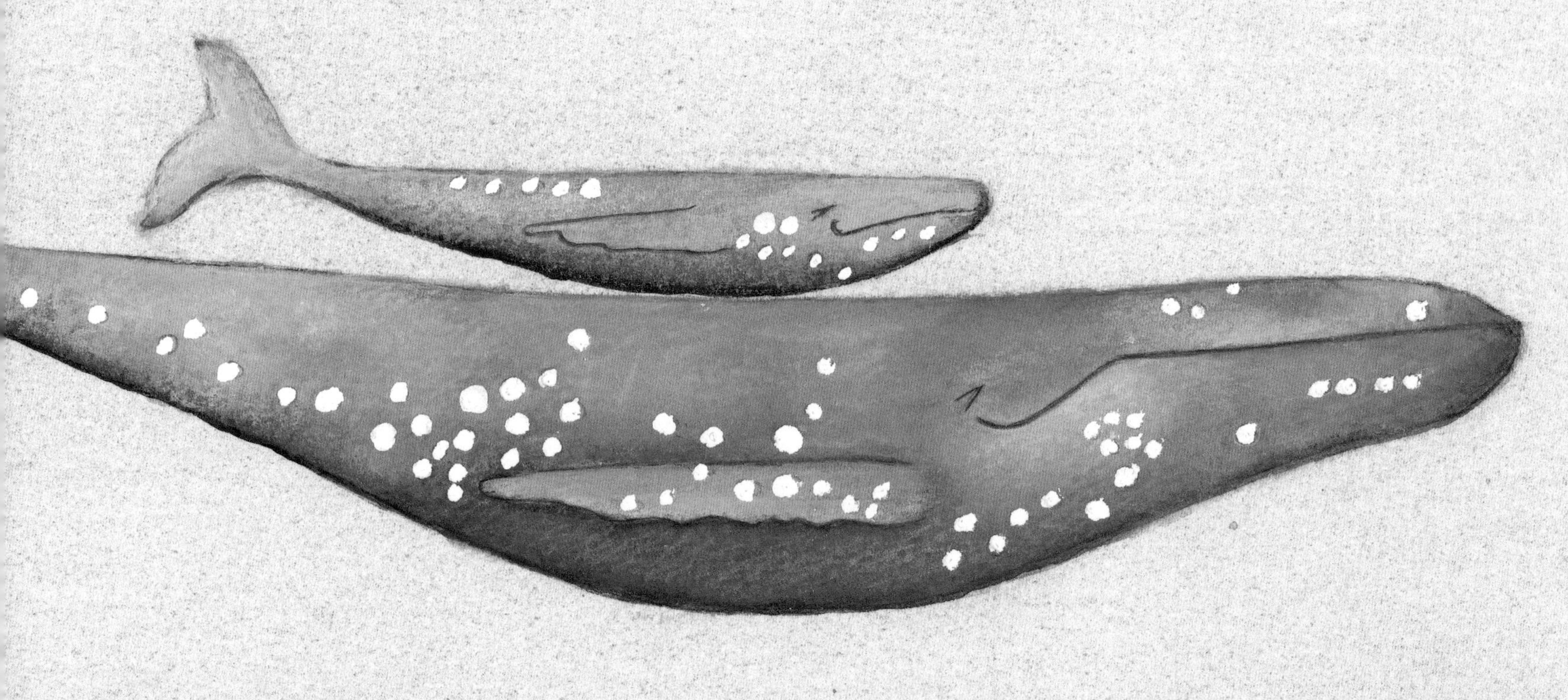

Briefly dozing *dugong* may
Rest her eyes by night or day.

*Lantern fish* so far from shore
Takes its rest on the ocean floor.

*Dolphin* baby in the deep.
Does he dream when he's asleep?

Safe from any stormy wave
Timid *moray* in their cave.

Gentle *seal* pup slumber deep
Could any baby be as sweet?

Now listen as the deep sea sighs
to sing your *Ocean's Lullaby.*